W9-BXY-873

## by Dr. M. Jean Greenlaw

Consultant:
Dr. Charles A. Doswell III
Doswell Scientific Consulting
NOAA Severe Storms Scientist (retired)

BEARPORT
PUBLISHING

New York, New York

**Credits**

Cover, © Wutthichai/Shutterstock, and © iStockphoto/Thinkstock; 4–5, © Dana Romanoff/
Getty Images; 6–7, © Le-Dung Ly/Science Faction/Corbis; 8–9, © Joe Amon/The Denver
Post via Getty Images; 11, © TORSTEN BLACKWOOD/AFP/Getty Images; 10–11, © Wang
Jianwei/Xinhua/Photoshot/Newscom; 12, © Andy Cross/The Denver Post via Getty Images;
12–13, © Thomas Cooper/Getty Images; 14–15, © Greg Sorber/Albuquerque Journal; 16, © The
Washington Times/ZUMAPRESS.com; 16–17, © iStockphoto/Thinkstock; 18–19, © Bodo Marks/
dpa/Corbis; 20, © Justin Sullivan/Getty Images; 20–21, © SABRINA LAURISTON/epa/Corbis;
22, © iStockphoto/Thinkstock; 23TL, © iStockphoto/Thinkstock; 23TR, © Tatan Syuflana/AP/
Corbis; 23BL, © iStockphoto/Thinkstock; 23BR, © The Washington Times/ZUMAPRESS.com.

Publisher: Kenn Goin
Editor: Jessica Rudolph
Creative Director: Spencer Brinker
Design: Debrah Kaiser
Photo Researcher: Picture Perfect Professionals, LLC

Library of Congress Cataloging-in-Publication Data in process at time of publication (2014)
Library of Congress Control Number: 2013038752
ISBN-13: 978-1-62724-129-8

For more information, write to Bearport Publishing Company, Inc., 45 West 21st Street, Suite 3B,
New York, New York 10010. Printed in the United States of America.

10 9 8 7 6 5 4 3 2 1

# CONTENTS

Floods . . . . . . . . . . . . . . . . . . . . . . . .4

Flood Facts. . . . . . . . . . . . . . . . . . .22

Glossary . . . . . . . . . . . . . . . . . . . .23

Index . . . . . . . . . . . . . . . . . . . . . .24

Read More . . . . . . . . . . . . . . . . . .24

Learn More Online. . . . . . . . . . .24

About the Author . . . . . . . . . . .24

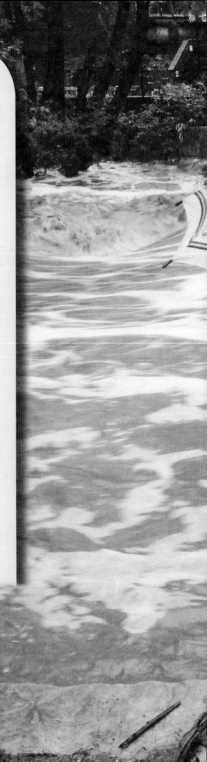

# FLOODS

*Boom!*

A thunderstorm begins.

Rain falls and water in a river rises higher.

A **flood** will soon cover the land!

Heavy rains and melting snow cause most floods.

100 YEAR LEVEL

50 YEAR LEVEL

Water spills over the river's **banks**.

It rushes over the land.

The floodwaters are everywhere!

During a flood, there's too much water. It cannot all soak into the ground.

7

Sometimes, it takes days of rain to cause a flood.

Other times, heavy rains cause a flood in just hours.

This is called a flash flood.

Flash floods may also occur when a dam breaks. A dam is a wall built across a river to hold water back.

Floodwaters rise very high.

They can cover a two-story house!

Water from floods ruins things inside buildings.

Sometimes, floodwaters flow fast.

The moving water knocks over trees.

It carries away cars!

Rushing water can travel 20 miles per hour (32 kph).

Floodwaters may trap people in houses or cars.

A person trapped in water can **drown**.

Rescue workers try to save people trapped in a flood.

6416775

15

How can you stay safe?

Listen to **weather reports**.

They will tell you if flooding is likely.

People who live near rivers or oceans are most at risk for floods.

If there is a flood, get to a safe place.

Go to higher ground or the highest floor in your home.

Then you can stay dry.

Some people put bags of sand near flooded rivers. This helps keep water away from buildings.

Over time, floodwaters soak into the ground.

It may take days or weeks.

Then the land is dry again.

After a flood, people clean up the mess left behind.

21

# FLOOD FACTS

- Floods can also be caused by strong storm winds that push huge ocean waves onto land.

- Rushing water can knock down power lines, so there may be no electricity during a flood.

- People who live in areas where floods occur should keep supplies like flashlights, canned food, blankets, and bottled water in their homes.

- People can drown if their cars get flooded. They should never try to drive on flooded streets.

# GLOSSARY

**banks** (BANGKS) the land along both sides of a river

**drown** (DROWN) to die from being underwater and unable to breathe

**flood** (FLUHD) an overflow of water onto land that is not normally underwater

**weather reports** (WETH-ur ri-PORTS) reports that tell what the weather will be like in the coming hours or days

# INDEX

banks 7
dam 9
damage 9, 11, 12–13, 20–21, 22
flash flood 8–9
floodwaters 7, 11, 12, 14, 20

rain 4–5, 8, 22
river 4, 7, 9, 17, 19
safety 16–17, 19, 22
weather reports 16

# READ MORE

**Chambers, Catherine.** *Flood (Wild Weather).* Chicago: Heinemann (2002).

**Koponen, Libby.** *Floods (True Books).* New York: Scholastic (2009).

# LEARN MORE ONLINE

To learn more about floods, visit
**www.bearportpublishing.com/ItsaDisaster!**

# ABOUT THE AUTHOR

Dr. M. Jean Greenlaw lives in Texas. She has written several books for children and contributed to textbooks.

**24**